XTREME JOBS

DAREDEVIL

BY S.L. HAMILTON

A&D Xtreme
An imprint of Abdo Publishing | www.abdopublishing.com

Visit us at
www.abdopublishing.com

Published by Abdo Publishing Company, a division of ABDO, PO Box 398166, Minneapolis, Minnesota 55439. Copyright ©2016 by Abdo Consulting Group, Inc. International copyrights reserved in all countries. No part of this book may be reproduced in any form without written permission from the publisher. A&D Xtreme™ is a trademark and logo of Abdo Publishing Company.

Printed in the United States of America, North Mankato, Minnesota.
052015
092015

 PRINTED ON RECYCLED PAPER

Editor: John Hamilton
Graphic Design: Sue Hamilton
Cover Design: Sue Hamilton
Cover Photo: Glow Images
Interior Photos: AP-pgs 4-5, 7 (bottom), 8-29, & 32; Corbis-pgs 7 (top) & 13 (inset); iStock-pgs 1, 2-3 & 30-31; Library of Congress-pg 6 (bottom left & right); San Diego Air and Space Museum Archives-pg 15 (inset); Wikimedia/Lapplaender-pg 6 (top).

Websites – To learn more about Xtreme Jobs, visit booklinks.abdopublishing.com. These links are routinely monitored and updated to provide the most current information available.

Library of Congress Control Number: 2015930949

Cataloging-in-Publication Data

Hamilton, S.L.
   Daredevil / S.L Hamilton.
   p. cm. -- (Xtreme jobs)
ISBN 978-1-62403-757-3
1. Daredevils--Juvenile literature.   I. Title.
796.7--dc23

                                                            2015930949

CONTENTS

Daredevil 4

History 6

Tightrope Walkers 8

Climbers 12

Wing Walkers 14

Air Show Pilots 16

Stunt Drivers 18

Motorcycle Stunt Riders 20

Animal Thrills 24

Job Facts 28

Glossary 30

Index 32

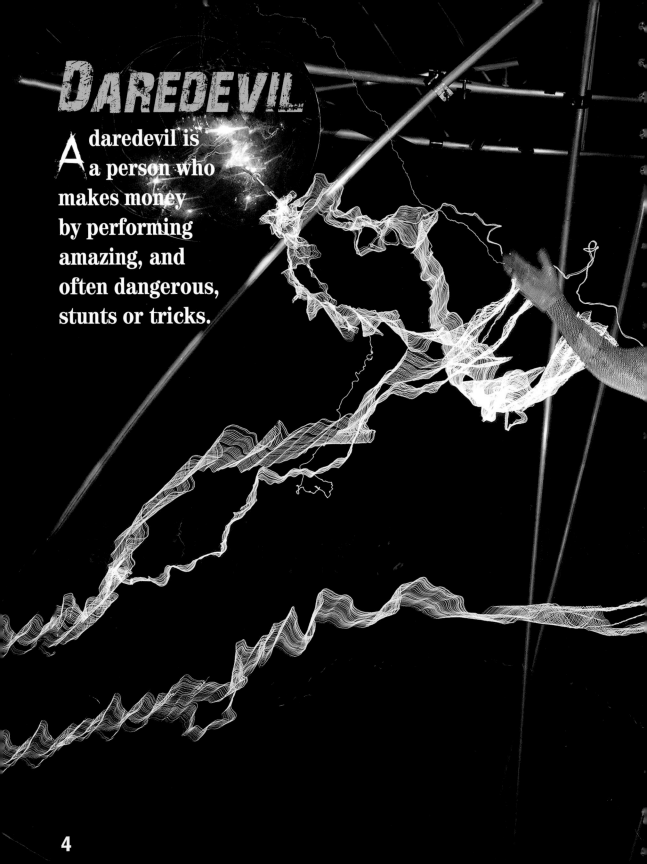

DAREDEVIL

A daredevil is a person who makes money by performing amazing, and often dangerous, stunts or tricks.

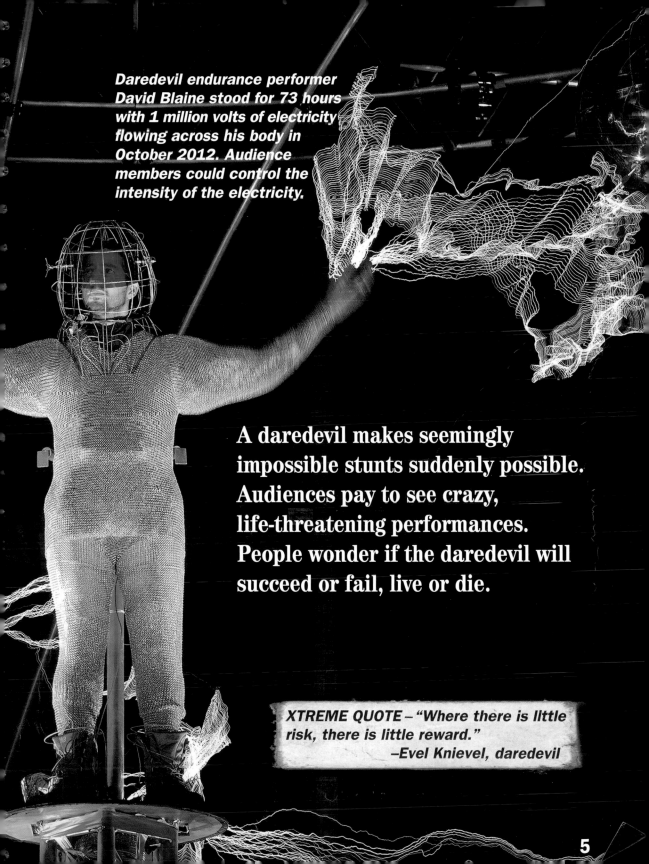

Daredevil endurance performer David Blaine stood for 73 hours with 1 million volts of electricity flowing across his body in October 2012. Audience members could control the intensity of the electricity.

A daredevil makes seemingly impossible stunts suddenly possible. Audiences pay to see crazy, life-threatening performances. People wonder if the daredevil will succeed or fail, live or die.

XTREME QUOTE – "Where there is little risk, there is little reward."
–Evel Knievel, daredevil

HISTORY

Daredevils have been thrilling audiences for centuries. An ancient painting shows Minoans bull leaping. Many daredevils performed in theaters or circuses. In the 1900s, audiences flocked to see death-defying stunts performed high in the air and speeding across the ground.

Daredevil acrobat and pilot "Fearless Freddie" Lund prepares to jump into a car driving just below him in 1921.

John Reynolds, better known as "The Human Fly," balances on a flag pole in 1924.

Hugo Zacchini becomes the first "Human Cannonball" in 1929.

Evel Knievel jumps 13 Mack trucks, setting a new record on August 20, 1974.

In the 1970s, Evel Knievel performed record-setting motorcycle jumps. His greatest attempt was jumping Idaho's Snake River Canyon in his Skycycle X-2 rocket. He failed, but survived. For many daredevils, broken bones and time in the hospital are a harsh reality, but daredevils love an "impossible" challenge.

TIGHTROPE WALKERS

For hundreds of years, daredevils have tempted fate by walking across a thin rope or cable suspended high above the ground. Tightrope walkers use balance and skill to keep from falling.

Nik Wallenda walks across Niagara Falls in 2012. With a TV audience of 13 million people, the network insisted he perform the walk with a safety harness against his wishes.

Today, millions of people watch in person and on television as daredevils perform their death-defying acts. Skywalker Nik Wallenda made history by high-wire walking across Niagara Falls in 2012 and crossing the Grand Canyon area's Little Colorado River in 2013.

XTREME FACT – *Tightrope walking is also called "funambulism."*

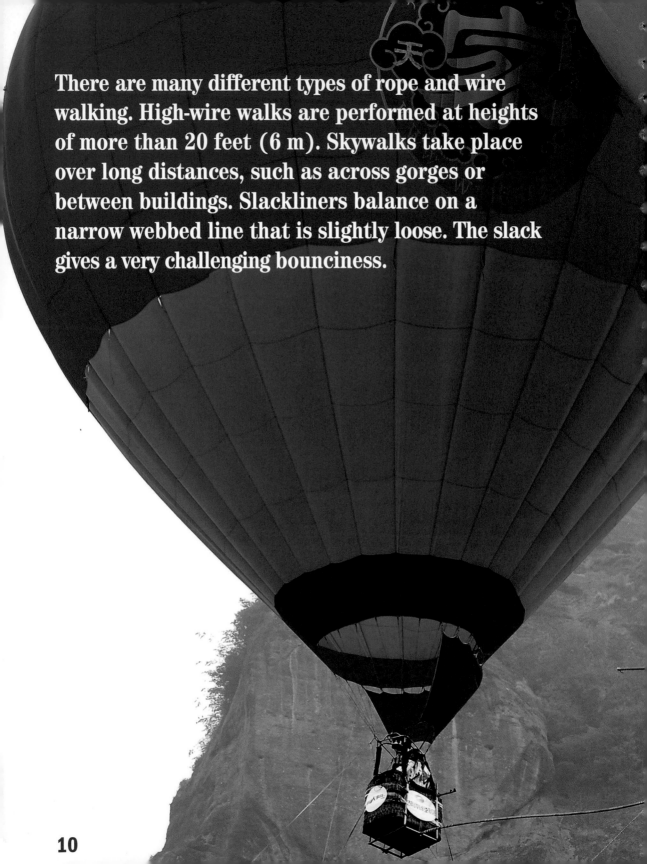

There are many different types of rope and wire walking. High-wire walks are performed at heights of more than 20 feet (6 m). Skywalks take place over long distances, such as across gorges or between buildings. Slackliners balance on a narrow webbed line that is slightly loose. The slack gives a very challenging bounciness.

All tightrope and slackline walkers learn their craft by starting close to the ground. Eventually, they work their way up to great heights. These daredevils have an excellent sense of balance. They are also calm under pressure.

Aerial tightrope walker Samat Hasan of China took only 3 minutes and 38 seconds to cross a 16.4-yard (15-m) high-wire that connected two hot-air balloons 33 yards (30 m) above the ground.

CLIMBERS

Daredevil climbers often have colorful names such as "The Human Fly" or "The French Spider-Man." They climb tall buildings, bridges, and monuments. Some perform without a net or safety harness. Some scale vertical walls without climbing gear. They use only climbing shoes and chalk for their hands. Climbers are often sponsored by TV stations or shows. They must get permits to legally climb in cities.

XTREME FACT– Urban climbers are people who climb for fun in cities. They are also known as "roofers." They often climb illegally and take photos of the city and themselves from the top.

Alain Robert, known as the "French Spider-Man," climbs the 950-foot (288-m) -tall Shimao Horizon Center Building in China's Shaoxing City in 2013. He also has scaled New York's Empire State Building, Chicago's Willis Tower, and the Petronas Towers in Kuala Lumpur.

WING WALKERS

The first airplane flew in 1903. About seven years later, the first daredevils began walking on airplane wings. Audiences were thrilled by the death-defying stunts. Many wing walkers were killed, but that didn't stop more daredevils from taking to the skies. Even today, trained pilots fly stunts with fearless daredevils on their wings.

Wing walkers at an air show in England.

Wing walkers often perform stunts such as handstands, dancing on the wings, and even jumping from one plane to another. They fly at speeds of about 100 miles per hour (161 kph). These brave daredevils earn their money by taking to the skies with a dose of showmanship madness.

XTREME QUOTE – "Safety second is my motto." –Ormer Locklear, World War I pilot and one of the first daredevil wing walkers

AIR SHOW PILOTS

Air show pilots perform incredible acrobatic tricks. These daredevils are experts at vertical nosedives, tumbles, spins, and flying just above the ground. Some are former military pilots. Others gain experience by working as crop dusters, commercial pilots, or freight carriers. To perform at air shows, pilots must pass a test given by the International Council of Air Shows (ICAS).

Air show pilot Skip Stewart passes just feet from the Shockwave Jet Truck during his daredevil act in Pensacola, Florida, in 2007.

XTREME QUOTE – "The most dangerous maneuvers are the ones people don't think are dangerous and vice-versa."
–John Cudahy, President of the ICAS

STUNT DRIVERS

Daredevil drivers jump, spin, ski (drive on two wheels), roll, and crash cars. They risk life and limb to perform explosive, glass-breaking, metal-crunching stunts. Driving skill, timing, and mathematical precision are needed to perform these dangerous acts.

Daredevil Spanky Spangler crashes his car into one of two buses standing on end. The domino effect stunt toppled both buses during Montana's 2008 Evel Knievel Days.

19

MOTORCYCLE STUNT RIDERS

Motorcyclists are known for their crazy daredevil tricks. They drive through fire, glass, and ice. They jump incredible distances. They wear protective helmets and safety clothing, but there are still many risks. Mistakes can result in bruises, blood, and broken bones. These daredevils must know exactly what their bikes can do under dangerous conditions.

> **XTREME QUOTE –** *"Anybody can jump a motorcycle. The trouble begins when you try to land it."*
> *–Evel Knievel, daredevil*

Motorcycle daredevil Clint Ewing speeds through the "Tunnel of Fire" in Sturgis, South Dakota, in 2013.

Some daredevil motorcyclists risk their lives racing in big, arenas. These barrel-like tracks have many names, including Demon Drome, Well of Death, Motordome, or Silodrome.

DEMON DROME

DEMON DROME

Riders roar only feet away from the audience. Speed holds the motorcycle onto the track. If the daredevil drops below a constant 30 miles per hour (48 kph), it's a fast and painful crash to the floor below.

To start and end their ride, motorcyclists use the ramped section at the bottom of the well to build up speed or slow down and stop.

↙

XTREME QUOTE – "I have nothing but respect for the slightly unhinged people who are prepared to defy gravity on old Indian Motorcycles..." –Back Street Heroes magazine

ANIMAL THRILLS

Some daredevils work with animals, both trained and wild. They perform stunts that amaze and often frighten audiences. Their work mixes human acrobatics, bravery, and foolhardiness with powerful, often unpredictable animals.

XTREME QUOTE – "If you're going to do something stupid, at least do it with confidence... just practice and be ready to do it."
–Fairland Ferguson, daredevil rider

Skilled horseback riders are called "equestrians." They can jump onto moving horses, ride backward, or even stand on a horse's back. Roman-style riders stand on two horses with one foot on each animal.

Fairland Ferguson mixes daredevil horse riding with acrobatics for her work in the 2013 show Cavalia.

Daredevil animal tamers risk death by putting their heads, hands, arms, or legs in the mouths of wild animals.

Serious injuries can happen when something goes wrong. Daredevils must be aware of a creature's habits. All animals must be cared for and well fed before a performance!

XTREME FACT – *An experienced Thailand crocodile tamer required 30 stitches to his face when his hand slipped on wet tiles while performing a head-in-the-mouth stunt. The startled crocodile snapped shut on the daredevil's head.*

JOB FACTS

Daredevils train for many years. This can mean a life of crashes, injuries, broken bones, and hospital stays. Some daredevils never earn regular wages. Others perform shows that pay an excellent salary. All daredevils enjoy the challenges, thrills, and excitement they receive by performing dangerous stunts for an amazed audience.

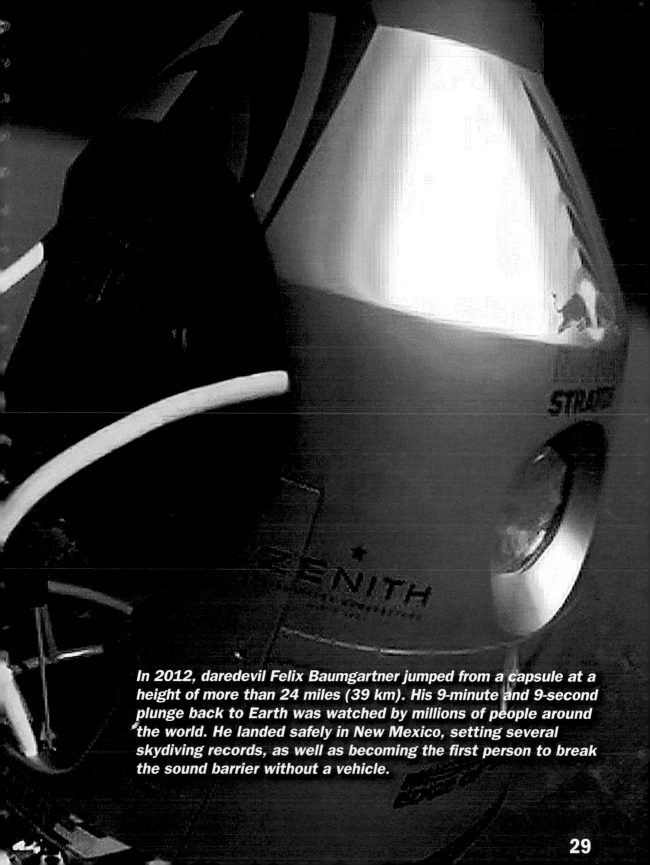

In 2012, daredevil Felix Baumgartner jumped from a capsule at a height of more than 24 miles (39 km). His 9-minute and 9-second plunge back to Earth was watched by millions of people around the world. He landed safely in New Mexico, setting several skydiving records, as well as becoming the first person to break the sound barrier without a vehicle.

GLOSSARY

Bull Leaping

A sport or religious ritual practiced by the ancient Minoan civilization. The bull leaper would either jump between a bull's horns and land in a handstand on the animal's back, or use the bull's horns to catapult himself to a standing position on the bull.

Crop Duster

A pilot who flies just above fields of crops and sprays them with a bug-killing solution.

Human Cannonball

A daredevil act in which a person is shot out of a cannon into a net, an inflated bag, or a body of water. Instead of gunpowder, the cannon is rigged with a spring or compressed air that catapults the person. Smoke, fireworks, and sound effects are added to make it seem like a real cannon. The greatest danger comes when landing. More than 30 daredevils have died performing this act.

INTERNATIONAL COUNCIL OF AIR SHOWS (ICAS)

A group founded in 1968 with the mission of ensuring that safety standards are met for air show pilots, sponsors, and audiences. To perform in an air show, a pilot must pass an ICAS certification test.

ROOFER

A daredevil who climbs roofs in cities, usually illegally. Roofers often perform death-defying stunts, such as hanging from the edge of a building. They also take photographs of themselves to post on social media.

TUMBLE

When an air show pilot makes his plane seem to tumble out of control, nose over tail or wingtip over wingtip.

INDEX

B
Back Street Heroes 23
Baumgartner, Felix 29
Blaine, David 5

C
Cavalia 25
Chicago, IL 13
China 11, 13
Cudahy, John 17

D
Demon Drome 22

E
Earth 29
Empire State Building 13
England 14
Evel Knievel Days 19
Ewing, Clint 21

F
Ferguson, Fairland 24, 25
Florida 17
French Spider-Man, The 12, 13
funambulism 9

G
Grand Canyon 9

H
Hasan, Samat 11
Human Cannonball 7
Human Fly, The 6, 12

I
Idaho 7
Indian Motorcycle 23
International Council of Air Shows (ICAS) 16, 17

K
Knievel, Evel 5, 7, 20
Kuala Lumpur, Malaysia 13

L
Little Colorado River 9
Locklear, Ormer 15
Lund, "Fearless Freddie" 6

M
Mack trucks 7
Minoans 6
Montana 19
Motordome 22

N
New Mexico 29
New York, NY 13
Niagara Falls 8, 9

P
Pensacola, FL 17
Petronas Towers 13

R
Reynolds, John 6
Robert, Alain 13
roofers 13

S
Shaoxing City, China 13
Shimao Horizon Center Building 13
Shockwave Jet Truck 17
Silodrome 22
Skycycle X-2 rocket 7
Snake River Canyon 7
South Dakota 21
Spangler, Spanky 19
Stewart, Skip 17
Sturgis, SD 21

T
Thailand 27
Tunnel of Fire 21

W
Wallenda, Nik 8, 9
Well of Death 22
Willis Tower 13
World War I 15

Z
Zacchini, Hugo 7